Kaleidoscopic Forests

Poems

Rune Kjær Rasmussen

ISBN: 978-99987-719-0-1

First printed 1 October, 2023
By RITONA
3, rue de Wormeldange
Rodenbourg, L-6955
Luxembourg
Editing, layout, and design by Ritona staff

For more information, see our catalogue and journal at
ABEAUTIFULRESISTANCE.ORG

Kaleidoscopic Forests

Poems

Rune Kjær Rasmussen

Within

Evening Sun

The last evening sun
gathers itself to become a drop,
more drops, many, many.

A storing and a charging takes place.

The cocoons are being shaped by the drops
out by the coast, and they can be seen
just by
squinting.

They come floating
like diving bells
but in the air.
Until they, with a few pauses,
stop, and almost crash down
to break the surface of the water.

A lot of them, almost all of them
should be left alone.
They are in the middle of processes
that do not concern humans.

They are situated somewhere
between resin and amber.
In a borderland with a different time.
And once in a while you are, yourself
within one of them.

It is cause for such a refreshing twitch inside me
when I land one morning
from a nightly chute
after having been inside
one of them.

During other mornings
a certain workforce
seems to be quite spent
but how and why
is quickly being covered
by heavy, black drapes.

The day always starts
with a specific fauna and flora
which is not up for discussion.
It makes it so wildly harmonic.

46

Went out to the ocean to find
out how it sets its boundaries.
It was my birthday.
I searched for the sand after the forest but
I only found a road called Forest Road.
Scattered trees. And in a glade
a playground. Someone was playing there. I was not.
I sat down on a bench, looked up, and started to breathe
in all the light green from the tree crowns.
Then I took off for a while.
I felt almost gluttonously fresh.
I also thought I might have been too greedy for a while
but in relation to music and since ownership of music
is impossible it was a whole other matter.
You cannot grab music, you can only use your arms, and other things,
as some sort of oars.

It is also a little bit sweet when someone presents
what they think they know
as a kind of loop they have not themselves seen yet.
A routine vocabulary.
One has to be careful with these sort of things.

Later that evening I received unwanted letters.
Something which should appear in a nice way, like a kind of life routine,
was so infinitely ugly and empty. It quickly led to me
putting a movie on.

The invisibility ointment

To be heard so little
the tongue felt dangerous in the mouth.
A foreign element tasting of more sedation.

To be seen so little that
the eyes only knew strategy
without the knowledge of this.

Like a narcotizing cream
against having skin.

A flash in a black sack in the shaft.

A small animal in the palm of the hand

That
which many recognize
but with its hesitating
language
like a small animal,
of unknown origin,
drinking
from the palm of one's hand.

This
is the reason
why the lines
change
like the shyness
someone carries around
for a long time
until they recognize that
it just concerns peace.

There is a new kind of graffiti in town

The unforeseen can be
the pigeon glimpsed in the corner of the eye
which has never been a pigeon
but a much larger gull
who is now looking up

with his what-do-you-want-gaze
in the middle of the pedestrian street.

The gulls are overtaking the town.
They have learned something new about the humans
and the ideas of monopoly
that are truly crumbling,
no, they are actually already long gone.

I recognize the anger in the gull's eye

and want to translate it.

Kicho

There was no doubt,
usually there often is:
The contrabass sounded so much like dark chocolate,
it was dark chocolate just in the form of sound.

The music could be tasted in the air,
there was a really strong cocoa
in those coarse vibrations
and it said,
among other things,
that
humans are much more romantic
than we often suggest.

To be romantic takes guts.
A re-reading of something that used to be
which some people only dare to call naïve.

Lines in tree, lines in chocolate.

Chocolate chips and sawdust
present themselves with a character,
no one could, no one can, hijack.

The double bassist was captain
on the ship of music.
Set sails on quick, fleeing,
impulses with
a concentration like when lightning strikes
and a love, with a subtle nut-like quality.

A minor theory about soundtracks

A minor theory appears:

that composers so finely can walk
on a beach
into a doubt
concerning
how to give presents, not least to one self,
an indestructible reevaluation
that clings round paradoxes,
hides in playful gestures
of wrapping, unwrapping,
seriousness attaching nights to days
when they get the chance to make music
for movies they will never forget:
when they burst out saying: I cannot

recognize myself in this ritual at all
and peace strikes in the most unexpected places.

In the schoolyard

A music box inside a snowball.
A blueberry inside a snowball.

To not identify one self as a barrel organ player.
Draw up a new study.

Remembering the old country maps which
with a staff
with a hook at the end,
was drawn down from up above the ceiling.

There was a formality to it
or perhaps I am dreaming that part.
We let go of those maps over and over
in the schoolyard.

Flying kites.
Ungovernable and
not at all flossed at the edges here many years later.
The thawing as a dragon cub.

In the living room

I embraced the harrowing in my living room.
It was a shy beast but untameable.
I held its shoulders.
It had to take the time it needed.
One day I knew it had turned into a tree.
A transparent tree.

And it was similar to that day,
where I almost called someone
who sits prepared for that sort of thing
to ask them
if I was wrong
about the construction of a single
glass building in every city in the world
that anybody should be able to enter
as well as being able to look into.

And I was most definitely wrong
but the thought of just asking a stranger
in an office somewhere in town
felt good.
I would ask:
Is this thought foreign to you?

Drawers

You can easily see the spot,
if you are familiar with that sort of thing.
The place where the class clown
drowned completely in irony.
It is marked with a little flag
as if in a dog turd
if it is marked at all.

My advice, to myself and everyone else
is to move on now.
Certain memories are
not much more than a rattle now.
Just a bit of broken toys causing a raised eyebrow.

What else are drawers for?

Missing authorities

Freedom is not chaos
in a destructive form.

The urge,
to place that sentence
like a soothing cloth
on the forehead of
a soul passing by,
pops up
like a jack-in-the-box.

But to give one self such authorities
has never been
and will never be
a good idea.

You cannot put your own experience
out for rent
in this way.

I do not throw a feather up in the air
for then to call it a bird.

I do not talk about movies I have never seen.

Freedom is not chaos

The ecosystems of music

Goes into hibernation with ideas about
finding the oldest instruments in the world
that gently change, arrange pillows,
small warm planets.

Looks peacefully at a sort of sleep bark
that protects my life with introvert seasoning,
not a cocoon
up for constant debate.

Does not consider those few times
a serious wound was repeated
as anything but a vague circle
in the surface of water.

Meditates for a long time over the names of instruments:
shakuhachi, duduk, koto, nyckelharpa
and gets lost in reverie barefoot
in a housecoat
on the stepping stones of memories.

Goes into hibernation
like a fresh swimmer inside the journeys
with all time available
behind a waterfall of opt-outs and peaceful flames
burning a focus clear: the music of the ecosystems.

Sun mirror

Silence from dark forests
floats in across shores.
Animals with no eyes lay down to rest.
In nests of longing waiting for a bridge.

The oceans keep an eye on the sky.
Whales disappear in a too small radar.
And the fishes gasp
as children who get an electric shock.

Gods lie freezing
on the edge of time
while goddesses keep
a clear eye on everything.

Sensations of transience
disappear in wells
while buckets are lowered down
through restless terrain.

Stop applauding
keep the hands still
above the bonfire the Sun
mirrors us in.

Stop performing
impressing and repeating
because this is the end
for each echo now.

Take the Sun in
and listen in this moment

seek shade where you can
instead of constantly wanting to cast it.

The night

The night is a big magnet.
The night is everything that has happened.

The blueberry plantation

The colors in the largest blueberry plantation in Denmark have a special glow.
When someone walks about picking the berries in the late hours of the day the
light is phenomenal. And it occasionally happens that the rain starts to fall
during that time. It falls surprisingly slow as if someone has done something to
time itself. Or times. One drop, one single early evening, stopped in front of
the eye of an 81 year old woman. She could, through it, see the parts of her
life which she thought she had forgotten. She was finally, for instance, assured
that what she always considered to have been a dream, wherein she had seen
an oak tree flourish, in fact almost explode, into numerous flowers, no one
associates with an oak tree, was not a dream at all but a glance into another
world she would soon step into. She took a handful of blueberries and ate
them.

An evening room

All the tears in the room of crying that I visit this night
are encapsulated in a naked bulb in the ceiling.
It waves inside it like smoke.

Later, while I am asleep, it is not improbable

that the bulb gets crushed by a force that comes
from I have no idea where and provides
a dream I would have never
asked for myself.

Mining

On the way to a concert with Huun-Huur-Tu
I passed by a shop named "Your New Friend".
It turned out to be a shop
that deals in diamonds.

During the concert I had to,
as it usually happens every time now,
hush on two men who acted more like
they had paid to experience themselves.

When they noticed my index finger
placed over my mouth
they agreed to be present
or at least quiet.

Their restlessness seemed like
diamonds rattling in the pocket
flickering shadows in front of a certain intimacy
now sold off in public.

Simple statement

I am not so good
at selling myself
because I am not for sale.

Jellyfish

It is said that jellyfish do not have brains
but a lot is being said. I have noticed that
some people seem to brush their consciousness about the world
with long monologues, serpentines which on a regular basis
are being blown out like tunnel spirals. Through them those ghosts
they cling to in theory, in practice, run.

Perhaps jellyfish are a type of brains in themselves floating around
in the ocean to protect the breath in the water and then release it,
when some teeny-weeny fish really needs it

The beaver

The beaver lay on its back, drifted along
hung out with nature in all its beaver-likeness.
The paws behind the neck, posing it seemed.
And, of course, I was thinking what it is like to
be a beaver because I really did not know what
it was like to be me, and it looked like
an impression to follow, and it reminded me of
days in my teenage room, where I also drifted away
in a daydream, where the pillows looked like stones
on the shore, and under the water at the bottom, where
the beaver scraped all time pressure away, and I was
surprised at how big the beaver was, it made me happy,
and I zoned out about this, to follow the beaver in the river
drift away so peacefully, it was refreshing,

it was a kingdom.

The sleep in wait

Sleep laying in wait
ready to get a hold of one
in the middle of a sentence
which otherwise was on its way
to something big
like the little wandering man
on the giant painting
at 'Filosoffen'.

Those without a voice

Those without a voice
are never without a voice
but in the middle of the absence
of a listener with no other motif.

Those without a voice
can quickly be burned
from getting under a magnifying glass
a little too close, may I blink now?

Those without a voice are
already piles of ashes
in the periphery of someone's thoughts:
non-existing mumbling wretches.

Those without a voice dream on occasion
about new types of invisibility
perhaps with a little fire, just fire, pieces of wood to throw in there
a certain soot up the arms, well-known smoke veils.

Those without a voice are too tired
to make use of their freedom of expression
because they know who shapes it, liquidates it
with money under the table and disturbing smiles.

Those without a voice are used to being subjected to violence
used to adjust a shield
a bag over the head on an already
dying conversation, a hole puncher, a wandering about.

Those without a voice can have strategies around sprouts
like small guards
they have not yet recognized as
not being hired by themselves.

Those without a voice are those
who get allotted a tiny fragment of freedom
a little foretaste of something which never happens,
in a small booth somewhere solitary.

Vague voice

Vague voice. Would like to tow myself as a child
up from a wishing well or myself, now, down, so
I would have had someone to talk to. With something
else than a vague voice. And an idea of a breakthrough
taken hostage, braided as knot. And not mistake
soft, but necessary, opt-outs with cut offs. I noticed
that I found peace by scratching myself and I got so tired
I was hoping for a substitute that never came.

Vague voice. Placing it gently in a nest.
Perhaps it is an egg. Perhaps just some tied rushes.
There is an elevator in the roots of time,
in the crowns of time. Vague voice together with an owl
in its cave. Why the darkness of a forest should be
scary back then I never understood. This moment
looking out through a movie shred, a blade of grass.

The harbour

Human relief was inside the egg of fear. As it cracked, a slow dancer came out asking the people passing by why they looked for a main character, as if life is a movie. The relief of being human was still a mystery. Just an added layer of strong vulnerability. There was a basement and a few pieces of furniture everyone could rent. The impossibility of a bunker in this world of wars replaced by a walk at the old harbour. Back when it was held in place by large rusty ships, that had not sailed for decades, maybe centuries and that fat anchor that no one could lift. No need to try. We watched the water and the shadows on the water, attracting drifters and dreamers with sketchbooks and notebooks, always a suddenly heavier bird becoming a word or a drawing. Clothing that felt like nests. Someone just jumped in the darkest of waters. We swam to the islands where the dancers all greeted us. We tried to impress each other with weird inventions, quicksand days. Sometimes it feels like pure luck to still be around. A bus driver once saved me from freezing to death. That sort of thing. Writing can be like quenching the thirst of a drawer, a bird in a nest.

Total rejection

Someone who does not acknowledge the existence of a tree
starts the moment after to talk about a god's
and should therefore, of course, just be totally rejected.

The cactus at the library

An unusually tiny librarian
moves around watering a huge cactus
that has been given a whole department to itself.
'Not to be lent out', it says on a note
glued to the jar.
Even that is necessary to point out.

It can take up to four days
to walk all the way around the cactus
and get it watered enough, but it is possibly
this librarian's favourite job.
The thorns are as beautiful as flashes
that have been frozen down
for a later event.

A rooster and a guinea pig

A black rooster, the name is Tosha, has been rescued, out of Mariupol by a woman. She says that she could not leave her friend behind, a friend surviving attacks on their mutual existence. And hunger. Hunger. Hunger. She has helped getting their mutual existence out of the city. And into a new hunger.

Another animal, a guinea pig, is seen on the run on a photo from Mariupol away from a human, who, perhaps, used to perceive it as a pet, a cozy little being in that person's eyes, in days that are now the past, not crashed into gravel but bombed to dust, unrecognizable in every way. The guinea pig has now become a potential source of food for the human. For the human to be able to survive but to what? The tiny legs hidden beneath the body looks like the gaze of the human on the picture. Scurrying. The desperation seems like something that could jump out of the picture in a physical form. Attack one with grief. To be attacked by grief carries with it its own kinds of sedation. Tools wrapped in ice. Fluttering arms under a doctor's white coat that is sticky. An attempt to interfere in a surgical way but interfere with chaos. The hopeless, but not completely hopeless because it moves.

I am reading that some people are trying to starve these other people in this city, Mariupol. Starve them to death. After having bombed the city to bits and pieces. They are called soldiers. Perhaps that is the right name. I do not know. Why do so few say that sentence nowadays? I do not know? It is certainly a fair ascertainment relating much.

I wonder who they are these people. For a moment I want to remove the title of human from them. As if that title involves something special, something noble, in itself. Humans. A word. Nothing else. I feel stupid when I do things like that. And then, after all, not.

I feel human. But do I know what it is? Yes. Shall I explain it? No. To be human is not an explanation you owe anyone.

A black rooster twists himself free from a shadow, almost buried he is free again.

- We must be sooted by this new hunger together. We must be sooted. Is my tongue a black stone in a stream? Is my tongue a black stone? Why does a collection of saliva increase around these people? A life with maelstroms and stepping stones is unworthy for everyone.

- But I am already full. I am disturbed in my peace. I do not seek it. I already have it. That peace is the foundation combined with the silence, its Siamese twin. They are merged at the roots. A double tree.
I am reading that a man and a puppy travelled 225 kilometers out of and away from Mariupol. His baseline was invisibility. Invisibility is necessary, a good strategy in a war. But in an invisible war, the kind that someone wants to lead against other people's lives because they feel too weak without spiritual clones, invisibility is just a door out and away from these freezing strategists. An offer concerning lightness without an anchorage in seriousness and gravity is an offer concerning exaggerated self-importance in an empty temple. What a nightmare: To become a self-appointed coach constantly in the process of inventing, using and consuming strategies as shields against life itself. To avoid that, to avoid them. Some stones with certain names on in the pocket. And the wonderful depths of the oceans.

I read and read. Maybe to be led to something that feels like a pile of soil in my hands. Or snow. I pad a little bit of snow back in its place.

Peace arrives in a street with snow. I sit with myself as a child in a snowstorm. I hold my own hand. Then we disappear together in the snowstorm. The child and I. I and me.

- You own your own story but could it be that it is under ice? Can you see your face behind ice? Do clouds sometimes feel like knives in your mind? Did someone manage to make you believe that you are not allowed to truly think? That you do not seriously own your own story? That you are under ice?

The next potato

The light yellow
from boiling
softened clod
and the sliding peel,
asymmetrical with the surface
from the satisfied bit,
so thin there seems to be
a lack of another word
for it
while the next potato
is taken up and eaten
stable provisions
the fingers feel safe
as handle
the taste discreet
but superb
a piece of jewellery in a fog
clinking softly.

Fossilized wood

The scent of fossilized wood surprises me.
This that it has a scent, surprises me.
Why, I do not know.

It moves me deeply. It is a wonderful scent.
And it is as if I forget it quickly again
every time I put the piece away.

An echo of something unexplainable
is then whirling around in the air like smoke
from way back but right now.

I will often place this fossilized wood
on my heart, my forehead
when I meditate in the future.

Unassailably strong
in all its tangibility.

The laundry room

I met a human
with such a contagious joy about
taking out and bringing home freshly washed clothes
from the basement.

It shaped a lightness in the attic
the whole building lived off for the rest
of the day.

Slid up like hands
in gloves
and gloves made of hands
while the dryer sang
with its fine neutrality.

Planes

A thunderstorm breaks out
in song.

A hole has been ripped in my blue
housecoat.

I am shortly thinking about the broken wings
of certain birds in the zoo.

The flapping circle of the clipped wings:
a cage in itself.

A museum for being tired
begins to break itself down.

The puncher of remembrance
would like to avoid the wings.

Something slimy and slippery
wants to writhe in mud.
Ghosts start washing
their clothes down by the stream.

Drops of melancholy
are watering their humanity.
Echoes hit the back
where the shoulder-blades mumble.
About wings, but wings on a broken plane.

And some deranged type
views himself as a pilot for others.

He is shouting something about a god
that should work as a parachute.

Let us all fall through the air together, he says
from the plane that must not even crash.

Then someone switches off a movie about a superhero
and it is certainly not hope.

Pig heads

A little more than ten years ago I told at a working place,
where I was an intern, that I had become a vegan. It did
not take many minutes before some man started talking
about when he was working in an abattoir and had joined in
with a group throwing cut off pig heads to one another, and
then he laughed out loud about this, apparently according to
him, jolly tale from real life.

But it did not escape my gaze how much his hands were trembling.
His violent arrogance quickly revealed itself as fear that tried to keep
away from itself. A bit like someone who constantly tries to scrape the
view from a window to throw it away. And pretend something crushed
cannot see itself.

Hands that hand themselves over

The hands on the skin and the skin on the hands and
the skin that hands itself over to hands. And the skin that burns
the skin of the skin and hands that burn
from what is being handed over. And the heat that runs parallel with transience
and transience that heats up the escape. And the fingertips
sharpening their sensations of tips against the fingers.
And the change that blooms from change to unfold itself to be able
to outfold itself. And the hands on the skin stroking the skin like
a hope. And the hair and the hairless and the contrast, swinging like a
pendulum
between one thing and another. And time
that curls up, stretches out and curls up again.
And the rubbing which rubs out the naked and the naked which
rubs the exact into place. And the shuddering refreshing itself
with new thirst and the thirsting refreshing itself with new thrills.
And the tongue against the tongue licking the sighs into shape. And
the sighs against the sighs longing for more.
A bulrush soft neck that bristles its brushes to be combed
while they are being combed by the fingers like flapping capes and
the folds between them. The genders and the sexes dream about being
swallowed
up by the genders and the sexes.

Dynamite liana

There was this one kiss
I will never forget
the taste like
a cotton candy grape
bursting

an explosive acrobat
delightfully suicidal
in the jungle of the senses

Buttons

They met in the elevator
sporadically but
it felt like every day
because some days
did not make much fuzz about themselves.

They shared a little music, fragments
like broken off icebergs, small codes
for something they never put into words
held the earphones up like buttons
someone had lost in the middle of rush hour.

Fly & Sun

Perhaps death itself consists of
a sort of organic material
one simply has to remove
like a speck of dust from
one's immortal spirit
a dead fly on the window
washed away by rain
except for one wing
through which one
can gaze directly into the sun.

Vanishing act

One day he just felt like dying from being untouched. He never asked for this education in loneliness, and he could not afford it anymore, so he did something he had never done before: He gave up.

While giving up he turned into a stone, a black stone with eyes. Then he closed his eyes. Apparently it was still time to hibernate and just fall with this new kind of gravity like a never ending waterfall.

He stopped asking questions, he stopped believing in crushed dreams like a kind of stardust and disappeared for a while to anyone but himself.

Peace stones

He knew which stones were the most peaceful, the ones most filled with
peace,
and every night he collected some of them as they had collected peace for
millions
of years from the wind, from beings passing by, gentle spirits and vital souls
cutting noise, and he put them in the soil near his house. They sprouted into
cliffs in his dreams at night, greeting certain waves, holding back other parts of
the ocean that had always ignored him, and he felt deeply at peace knowing
that
he would leave the foam alone.

A man with a lot of experience concerning his own ways with the wind

Occasionally
a man in the room
a man as old as the city itself
so it seems
time itself in the city

he must go forward, onwards
he falls, now on the floor
still sliding forwards
at the library
I see him there

at the bus stop one day
I lent him an arm, it was just an arm
a boost, a little nudge
I noticed level-headed
This man is so tired, he is
so tired
if something is obvious
to anyone
it is that
but a mentor he is
of time

he must go to the library
read the papers he must

he lets the slightest
whirl him a little further
he walks with his walker
everyone and everything a kind of walker now
or a handle and a thank you
bursts from him

re-arrange, move a gaze, re-focus
sit at a table
newspaper a sheet of notes to just barely
follow the latest news
the latest news

every morning he finds
the energy of that day
a pointer, a bookmark
the reasonable route
while the memories are his own.

The forgiveness rack

There you go
with your forgiveness rack
in front of you.

A mirror has been installed.

It clatters and rattles
but never breaks.

It is quite a monstrosity
and there are struts in it
as in a kind of corset.

The forgiveness like a short cut
A designed flash.

And the slapdash darkroom
you fold out with the arms.

With a little spit on

Streams were being corrected.
And teeth. Someone had to talk
through a grid for years.
Inconvenient bark
was being scrubbed off of
a little too angry bones.
Some sat in camps,
others around a campfire.
It was a matter of queue culture
and those who already had the funds
should come first.
Then they handed the leftovers
already thoroughly chewed
and with a little spit on it
a sort of dressing
someone said to someone
under the table
with a funny look
apparently generous in their own eyes.
They wanted to correct streams
as they wanted to correct teeth.
In all cases management was going to happen.
It was an unwritten, but in practice always made,
law. And the individuals who had never joined
in the prescribed way or even thought about it
were already perceived as someone who left,
possibly someone
to earn a little more money on
or push out some further entertainment from
before the taxi arrived again.

The fruit bearer's vacation research

My work bears my fruit.
When I tell myself that I
should have a vacation, I often
start to seriously work.
The paradox of freedom.
To set one self free:
To gamble with one self.

Is fire your favourite haunting?

You have to be alone
for a long time
to see if you are one
who is suitable for that
you have to be alone
for a long time
to see if you think
loneliness is an illusion
or not.

Freedom is lightning
creating ghosts or rather
wringing them free
from rocks, freedom is lightning
creating ghosts
who will haunt themselves
until the house is burned down.

You have to be alone
for a long time
to see if you are a flame
suited to be that.
You have to be alone
for a long time
to see if you think
fire is a worthy
haunting of yourself.

Foundation of experience

Does the sea collect experience from the drowned?
Of course.

When I sail the sea
I can be so lucky
to understand that each wave crest,
each spray of foam, is an experience
being exhaled in an infinitely mystical
and endlessly moving, kaleidoscopic
cycle.
The understanding is a breath.

The experience of the ocean embraces my mind.
Back when I drowned I was there
with a sacrifice.

Earth's foundation of experience.
smiles
with gazelles.
The back of a hand, a ridge.
Contagious.

My foundation of experience
pinches itself
in the arm
rushing after itself.

I put up a parasol
in yet another transient comfort zone.
A new way of letting the shadows
fall.

Do you have enough experience
with your experience?
Do we?
The paradoxical forces of time.
The uncertainty in a potential.

I listen to chamber music from Lithuania.
It can be listened to in other places than just Lithuania.
Luckily enough.

Music is not philosophy.
Akira Ifukube noticed that.
A foundation of experience without music
is a sketch.
A self-overestimating will believe
that now it is just time for interpretation.
The point of orientation that has not discovered
a certain kind of double quicksand
flowing in an endless starry sky
and a gigantic net of roots
is like a conductor in front of an orchestra pit
without an orchestra.
Though, there is here
a certain chamber without limits

wisps of clouds as mitts.
The creamy silence of the senses.

A gesture.
Coconut milk and pineapple rings.
The dissolving, uplifting humility of music.

And those moments where one's own foundation of experience
seems to lighten up someone else's inner longing.
That immediate contact, you never forget that.
When something suddenly knows that it is inviolable.
And the only longing left is the longing to be as close as possible
to the music.
The loudspeaker as a heart muscle.

When the silence between you and me makes us visible in this way
instead of invisible.
The different nuances of hesitation in the music.
The sorting out in the instruments.
There is no us and them. Only you and me.
Certain 'political projects' sound like attempts to maintain
deserts as protected areas for golf and agreeing on the monetary value of
gold.
The speakers because of this often sound like endless desert walks of spin.

Now the drowned get up from the sea.
It is in another dream
but the evil dream has lost.
Eventually that with no vision always does
because it cannot even see itself in the world.
Earth's foundation of experience takes care of that.
Like removing hair from a brush.

The eggs of turtles are hatched
and they swarm out into the sea.

There is not a single hungry ghost
between them.
Each shell looks like a written sign.

One day we will not remember each other.
We have to remind each other of that.

Eyelashes as hands of a clock

The stunning in the infinite.
Eyelashes as hands of a clock
attacking cycles
in a different manner.
Encapsulating moments in
the most life-affirming ways.
All the forests that will ever exist
in one single gaze. It was there, and then it was
gone.

The hearts of the ocean

There has been some calcification
in parts of the ocean's hearts.
They used to beat uninhibited, untameably
on the seabeds everywhere in the world
and send out streams of vital blood,
transparent and therefore even more
fantastic, through all the veins of the oceans
but they are waiting for new operations
with their percussion against pollution
and doing so in their own time.

Animals

The shadow of someone's time is crumbling.
A little food for the ducks. In a park that slowly
but surely closes in on its own rituals.

Someone has forgotten what they dreamt of the first time
they met in the park. They dreamt of turning into foxes.
There was some envy in the air concerning the development
of the thicker fur in the winter.

One asks: Have you had a talk with the animals you envy
today? You have to develop a language before you can
seriously talk about and with them.

Imagine all the language you do not know about.
Hibernating everywhere around the world. Or in full speed. The claws
and the paws and the grabbers. The elements. Sunshine
finding its way to a snout, a pinecone, a beetle.

What kind of word is an animal to give to so many?

In what way is your envy within you? Is there an uncertain
skill flickering in your immediate surroundings? Are you unable
to really get to it? And do you really think that you can at some point?

Do you make a flag wet by dipping it in your own
blood? Are you a flag swimmer or a free diver?
When do you think you have not dreamt at all?
Can you feel your lips? What do they want now?
A new species is discovered every day and another one dies.
It never stops.

The tool with which the grace of cranes is measured

A powder
made from that tool
the grace of cranes
is measured with

once upon a time it was a spoon
to both stir in and
throw the stars out with

and it is also just someone
clearing their throat
in the waiting room
at the doctor's

the shyness of a toad
now as
lump
in the throat

all those coughs
like knots
from sawn off
branches

the strange beetles
of the past running
over the back of the hand
and out

Bridges

Responsibility drips down between the impossible
and what we expect before we look around.

There is a very special quality to the bridge
between late summer and early spring.

It is impossible not to fall through.

It looks stable though from far away
like those promises one as a child gave to thunder.

Strong green cardboard

I went up against the wind walking with four pieces of strong green cardboard,
or they were in fact rolled together and I could not stop myself from
singing a bit between that tube, with the pedestrian way pretty stable under
my
feet, the acoustics was not bad at all although more fleeing than in a lounge,
naturally, and I thought about whether there at some point back when you
were
a baby was an assumption that all stones were sweets to be tasted, that those
too could be devoured in that way through one's own organism with a little
patience and I thought about something like I do not believe that anyone as
such ARE geniuses but that there exists a possibility to surrender in an
inscrutable way to a sort of world genius, if the circumstances are right, if you
yourself pad a bit on the shoulders when the suitable sand castles are ready,
oh well, you think so much, and you should, do not believe anyone who says
there are things you should not think about because who does not like, and
need, to be thought of?

Sun leaves

One day I sat on a bench besides Odense Å
a stream that runs through the city
where I currently live
and I saw how the light
from the sun
ribbed and waving in the water
was reflected in
the lowest hanging leaves of a tree
by the shore.
At first I thought that the light
hit the front side of the leaves in an,
to me impenetrable way
after I had twisted and turned the possibilities,
but then I understood that the light
hit the backside of the leaves and
because of the force in the light
and the transparency of the leaves
it created a beautiful,
almost hypnotic, movement
a constantly changing, rolling
movement in the leaves
and parts of them,
that hung, temporarily
in the exact angle
in relation to the light.
A thought about the leaves
being somehow magically oxygenated,
soaked all the way through by fresh sap
occurred to me.
It was at the same time

a very moving and very calming vision
and that vision, that experience,
I find resemble the experience of listening to

the compositions of Justė Janulytė.

Gaia's nemeton

It is possible that there is a kind of saved energy in stones or clouds, for instance, which then in a still inscrutable way has been released and caused those few examples of dance mania that we know of. A sort of defense mechanism which can be called a spiritual seed from nature's side. One more. Gaia's nemeton.

Maybe.

The mystery surrounding how the energy gets in there and is being stored is also exciting. The dance does, no matter what, have an oxygenating perspective. And effervescing through every cell. Kaleidoscopically instead of focusing in an illusionary way. It is not free imagination but imagination as authority. Not without scruples because there is hesitation but hesitation before snow like a careful foot.

The hare and the roe deer

The recollection of the hare and the roe deer
sneaks unconcerned into a waiting room.
They came running towards the same point,
and then they stopped, like frozen in an instant,
on the spot, when they caught each other's eyes.
Perhaps it was a form of immediate meditation
one that both hares and deers practice.
The view was enough to save lots of future days
just through the readiness of
being able to be rewinded.
A form of recollection's net of roots
like a safety net beneath you,
stretched out a long time ago.
Something indestructibly wonderful like Earth.
If Earth ever disappears from here,
it will have found a way to clone itself before then.
What Earth really wants does in fact demand
something eternal, I am sure of that.
Something eternal that breathes
through right now.

The blurred takes care of itself

The lifelong study of life
which in moments opens up eternities
when all senses are used
is dragged up, out, from the light silt
and the experience shivers in every root
the self shakes itself wilder,
one more time more untameable
with nights folding their black wet
mouths around the consciousness.

The forests

There is water in the trees
and blood in my body.
Sometimes at night
we exchange these liquids.
Not out of envy but respect.
A necessary operation.
Sleep's mystery.

I go to the forests and ask:
Do you come out to play?
To play is to learn. No.
To play is to learn to play. No.
To play is to play.

Why do some highlight confusion
with such strange
self-proclaimed accuracy?
As if there is a constant quake
in all worlds, all dimensions.
Peace may be all there is.
Or darkness. A kind of dark peace.

The world makes so much sense
there is no reason to try to
reduce it
and call it otherwise.
The sun casts no shadow.
Sometimes the sun is
dreaming of the forests.

The forests hold
all longing in this world.
You should go in there,
or otherwise you will be
thrown in there
and you will miss a step,
two steps, more.
It is very easy to miss a step.

Dance.

You can put your ear
to an acorn.
There are children's songs inside it.
And not just those of human children.
Of course not.

Old acorns occasionally
become conchs.
It is a mystery.
Or, well actually it is just words,
the fox says.
When everything else seems to fail,
you can believe the fox,
the way the fox moves.

Your mind is kind of like
an infinity in the soil.
I had to stop singing
for a while
and just be silent
in the forests.

To find a new transparency
in the roots.
There is generosity
in every net.
There are fishes made of soil down there.
They swim in different ways,
in different dimensions.

There are fragments of memories
in the forests.
The forests are a way for the world
to explode.

If you walk through a forest
enough times
the forest will get you to know you more.

Sometimes in your life
you must be alone
even for a long time.
Then ask yourself:
Am I truly alone
among these trees?

Astronauts do not care
about the forests.
They want to find life that is
very similar to themselves
but far, far away.
They have a telescope and a microscope
and they are not sure how to use them.
Maybe they are trying

to make a ring.
Show me yours and I'll show you mine,
they seem to say.
Is there life on other planets? they ask.
Ignoring so much right in front of them.
All around them. Down in the underground.
Up in the sky.

Your eye is an egg that hatches
again and again in the forests.
Your mind is not a diamond that can crack
like an egg to replace or explain the worlds.

Kaleidoscope removes focus.
Replaces it.
If you do not focus kaleidoscopically
maybe your focus is just a comma.

Sometimes there is a man in the forest
who looks like someone who would like
to think some special thought that would
guarantee his resurrection.
But he will soon be gone.
He cannot understand
the patterns in the leaves.
When he tries, he dies.
There are many creatures in the forests.
Some of them have lived there all the time.
Others are newcomers.
Some are what is called extinct.
They live underground now, in the roots.
Or up in the air.

Some prefer that.
They hibernate in different ways.
No one can truly die because there are
laws against that. Natural laws.

I saw a soldier in the forests.
He was so scarred.
His life like a big tattoo
he could not get by.
He wanted his tent to be flames.
He wanted the forests
to somehow cremate him.
He looked like someone
who had finally given up on
collecting weapons.

Time has a special place
in the heart of the forests.

I was once rejected by a forest
after ignoring my self-respect.
I got a rash so bad I had to leave
itching and scratching myself all the way home.
Never before or since have I had one like that.
It is not a metaphor, it is true.

If you are in a hurry
you will never be in the forests.
The animals in the forests are the forests too.

To be here is to be clear.

The forests can deal with everything.

You cannot cultivate them.
They will cultivate you.
They work with your memories.
They turn them around like mobiles.

If I were to say I was a devotee of
anything or anyone
I would say I am a devotee
of the forests.
Sometimes when there is nothing else to do
I go to the forests.

Run through the forests,
walk through the forests
or sleep in the forests.

The music of the forests can be very subtle
but there is always music.
Even the silence
is just music hibernating.

You are potentially mine, the forests say.
Eventually you will be.
The forests are storage rooms as all bodies are.
Like you are.

Sometimes, unexpectedly,
a tree will open like a fan
to make you live in a cool breeze of comfort
for a while.

It can happen during the night
or the day but always
while you are dreaming.
When are you not dreaming?

The forests welcome the abused,
the neglected, the hidden
and the hopeless.
The forests welcome the tender
and the soft,
the scared and the crumbling.
Sometimes the forests look at you
as a sacrifice.
Sometimes forests need to heal themselves
and you must leave them alone.
If you do not, you will learn a lesson.

Sometimes, but not often,
you find someone to fall in love with
in the forests.
It can be very quick,
just a glimpse in a stream or a wet leaf.
The moon has a wild, wonderful face
which reflects back here.
I am very healing to be with,
but a lot of people want to abuse it
so I tend to stick to myself, a few
others and live inside this tree,
a spirit of the forest came by and said,
quickly vanishing again.

When squirrels fall in love,

acorns are smiling.
It is a true story.

There is no end or beginning to the forests.
That is what is so baffling about them.
They cheat death.

A bed of ferns dedicated to silence in forests

Life is so filled with meaning it is meaningless
to try to reduce it.
Silence in forests is different than silence in other places.
Silence in forests is a state of mind to seek into.
A state which does not demand anything recognizable.
A place to step out into.
When I seek out the forest I seek out the end of my own,
immediate, verbal language
and step into the start of something different, something that
celebrates the potential, the green,
that which oxygenates in a cycle,
that which simply wants to blink
in front of forest floor,
bark and moss,
in front of a vital connection
that is not tangled up in anything.

On a bed of ferns I place everything I know to see it disappear
into everything I do not know.

About The Author

Rune Kjær Rasmussen is an animist, writer, singer, and occasional painter from Denmark.

About Ritona

RITONA is the imprint of Ritona a.s.b.l, a not-profit organization advocating for pluralism, tolerance, and respect for Pagan, Indigenous, and non industrial ways of being in the world
Find our works at abeautifulresistance.org